How to Boost Your Creativity

I0482264

HTeBooks

Copyright © 2016

Copyright © 2016 HTeBooks

All rights reserved. This book or any portion thereof may not be reproduced or used in any manner whatsoever without the express written permission of the publisher except for the use of brief quotations in a book review.

Disclaimer

This book is designed to provide condensed information. It is not intended to reprint all the information that is otherwise available, but instead to complement, amplify and supplement other texts. You are urged to read all the available material, learn as much as possible and tailor the information to your individual needs.

Every effort has been made to make this book as complete and as accurate as possible. However, there may be mistakes, both typographical and in content. Therefore, this text should be used only as a general guide and not as the ultimate source of information. The purpose of this book is to educate.

The author or the publisher shall have neither liability nor responsibility to any person or entity with respect to any loss or damage caused, or alleged to have been caused, directly or indirectly, by the information contained in this book.

Table of Contents

How Will This Book Help You?

In today's modern creative economy, one of the most critical skills to possess is being creative. People who are creative are marked by their dedication to their craft, their patience, their ability to think outside of the proverbial box, and their willingness to take risks. These traits are essential not only in completing artistic pursuits, but also in forging greater happiness in your life. The succeeding chapters discuss in greater detail why creativity is important and what you can do to become a creative person yourself.

5

Lending Appreciation to the Value of Creativity

"Others have seen what is and asked why. I have seen what could be and asked why not."

– Pablo Picasso

If there is a glaring pitfall in the current pedagogical system used in educational institutions across the country today, it is the fact that it leaves very little room for students to develop creativity. Most of the time, students are subjected to rigid school policies that prevent them from veering from the established curriculum or else face stiff penalties from school administrators.

Instead, students are taught to toe the line and finish their studies so they can automatically be aligned to a predefined future. This future, more often than not, involves being a lifelong employee to giant corporations, building a domestic life, growing old at a retirement community, and finally passing away. Nowhere can the emphasis on creativity be found in this preset timetable.

The lack of focus on fostering individual creativity can pose problems in the long run, especially in light of the emerging creative economy. Where once the focus used to be on manual labor before it gradually shifted to industrialized operations, these days success can be had by those who can present the most creative solutions to modern industry problems, including design, e-commerce, engineering, communication, and finance. In other words, at no other time is the ability to think outside of the box more pressing than at the current period.

A life of creativity

But being creative and exercising it in your day to day life need not be grand or life-changing. In fact, creativity is something that can be applied even in the most mundane or quotidian of situations. For instance, whiling away time at a cafe waiting for your friend to arrive can be spent writing or sketching. At the subway, being observant and mindful of your fellow passengers can yield the much-needed inspiration you need for your next creative project.

The key is to develop the tools needed to exercise creativity as part of your lifestyle. While some people may seem naturally inclined to be creative in their endeavors, take heart in the fact that creativity is a skill that can be learned over time.

The succeeding chapters highlight the traits that mark a creative individual and what you can do to kick start a life of utter creativity.

Today's creative economy calls for greater individual creativity.

Identifying the Traits of a Creative Individual

"Creativity is a habit, and the best creativity is the result of good work habits."

– Twyla Tharp

Many people are discouraged from exercising creativity in their day to day lives simply because they refuse to acknowledge their capacity to be creative themselves. Often, you will hear them say, "But I'm not an artist," or "I don't have it in me to be creative," as if one is born either with or without creative genes.

But the fact is, the biological component of creativity is one that is still subject to greater tests and studies. In the meantime, creativity should not be treated as a genetic trait, but rather as a skill that you can acquire through education and practice. In other words, with discipline and an ample amount of will, anyone can be a creative individual.

There are a number of traits that distinguish a creative person. These are the same traits that shape and define their capacity for greater imagination, which they use either in their everyday tasks, their work, or in their spare time. Some of these traits include the following:

Creative people are naturally curious.

If you want to develop your creativity skills, you would need to be mindful of everything around you because each little thing corresponds to a certain meaning or symbol. Being curious means you do not merely take interest in something, you also take concrete actions to turn this thing into something novel. Part of this trait is the ability to ask questions: what does this thing stand for? How is it meaningful? What can I use it for?

Creative people are willing to try out new experiences.

You shouldn't be limited by your existing knowledge and experience. Creativity calls for constant growth and development. Learning and relearning things is an integral part of unleashing your potential to create. If you are into visual arts, for example, you should be well-versed with different styles, brush strokes, and painting techniques. It is only by studying these different facets of painting will you discover your own unique style.

Creative people are patient.

While it is generally understood that creative people have a lot of ideas running in their heads, they are also the first to acknowledge that they can only do one thing at a time. The only way to finish a project is by sporting patience and commitment to it. Otherwise, you end up with piles of unfinished works that do not at all convey what you wish to express. For writers, this means enduring the often laborious process of researching, writing a draft, editing, and proofreading before finishing a written output. Despite the volume of work involved, it's best to consider the finished output as the reward to all your labor.

Creative people are goal-oriented.

Sure, you may have a sudden burst of creativity, enough for you to sing, dance, paint, or write. But despite their sporadic nature, these little acts of creative expression form a part of the bigger picture, which includes your goals of becoming better at what you are doing. Each thing you do reinforces these goals. So if you find yourself sketching a portrait, for example, you know this is part of your bigger goal of becoming a better visual artist.

Creative people think outside of the box.

This is what separates ordinary thinkers from creative thinkers; the latter do not confine themselves within strict and dogmatic restrictions. They are compelled to see things from a different angle, not for the sake of being different, but to underscore the fact that there is more than one way of looking at things. Mastering this skill is indubitably a hallmark of creative people.

Creative people are willing to take risks and are unafraid to fail.

Fear of failure and of the unknown is one of the reasons that hampers the creative growth of many people. If you aspire to be more creative, you should be able to overcome this debilitating fear. The succeeding chapters will discuss in greater detail some strategies that you can subscribe to in order to be more fearless and daring as you develop your creative skills.

Creativity is a skill that can be learned over time. Some of the traits creative people share include being naturally curious, sporting intense dedication to their craft, and having the ability to think outside of the box.

Identifying the Challenges that Hamper Creative Growth

"Great minds discuss ideas. Average minds discuss events. Small minds discuss people."

– Eleanor Roosevelt

Before proceeding to the discussion of what you can do to boost your creativity, it is important to first identify some of the most common challenges that hamper your creativity. The point is to understand where these problems are coming from and what you can do to eventually overcome them.

The chief obstacle to creativity are self-doubts and insecurities. Being creative calls for confidence and a semblance of self-assurance. If you are perennially on your toes because of imagined monsters, it would be very difficult to sport an openness to ideas—something that is doubtlessly crucial in the creative process.

Most insecurities come from unresolved issues in the past. Take a step back and try to figure out the root of your fears. Did you grow up in an environment where you were constantly called out for every little infraction you've committed? Were you subjected to intense pressure growing up? Were you bullied by your peers? Did you grow up thinking you don't have anyone whom you can fully trust?

These sort of issues obviously take time to heal. Often, however, the first step in coming to terms with your past is in acknowledging it. There's no point in trying to forget things in your past as if they did not happen. They did. The more you deny them, the more these ghosts will haunt you.

Doing away with self-hate

Another factor that hampers creativity is excessive self-criticism. It is totally fine to be self-critical, but not to the point where you fail to find anything satisfying in yourself. Excessive self-criticism is almost paramount to self-hate. And if there's anything you should do, it is to learn how to love yourself. The sooner you learn to accept your limitations and weaknesses, the easier it becomes for you to take steps to better yourself.

Complacency is when you are not doing anything to improve your knowledge or your circumstances in general. You are so used to the current set-up, so much so that you avoid changing anything in your life. As far as creativity is concerned, this can be a bad thing, especially since being creative requires a certain degree of dynamism.

But the greatest obstacle, perhaps, to fostering creativity in your life is the fear of failure. When you are afraid of committing mistakes, you provide yourself very minimal chance to grow and learn. This fear will be discussed in greater depth in the next chapters.

In order to foster greater creativity in your life, you need to overcome the challenges that hamper your creative growth. Some of these challenges include insecurities, excessive self-criticism, tendency to be complacent, and fear of failure.

Creating a Sense of Self-Awareness

"Passion is one great force that unleashes creativity, because if you're passionate about something, then you're more willing to take risks."

- Yo-Yo Ma

It's not enough that you are creative merely for the sake of being creative. Far more important is your ability to channel your creativity in creating something tangible and real. Without the actual creation process, your creative skills will remain in your head and will not therefore be fully consummated.

On this end, it is necessary for you to sport a sense of self-awareness in order to identify the things that you are passionate about or deeply interested in. Knowing what your passions are will allow you to put your creativity to good use because then your actions will be dictated by clear and specific goals. This way, you do away with random activities that do not serve any real purpose over the long term.

For some people, for example, photography counts as one of their passions. Most ordinary camera owners would just point and shoot with little regard for such technicalities as aperture, shutter speed, or the rule of thirds.

Deliberate, not accidental

But creativity calls for something more than the usual. If you are serious about photography, it is incumbent upon you to exercise greater creativity with each shot you take. In this sense, your photos become deliberate outputs of your creativity, with due attention to the technical details that other people wouldn't normally pay attention to. Your photos are not merely accidental, and this is precisely what lends them greater depth.

This sense of self-awareness should not just apply to your strengths. You should also have a clear idea of what your perceived weaknesses are. This will allow you to work on them in the hopes of turning them into strengths, or at the very least will instruct you about the limits of what you can do.

On the same note, get rid of distractions. More than anyone else, you should have an idea of what your potential distractions are. Do you get easily distracted by email or SMS notifications on your phone? Then turn it off or put it on silent mode while you are engaging in a creative exercise. Do you get distracted by cable news channels? Then turn off the TV, or better yet, get it out of your room.

In sum, the more self-aware you are, the more manageable it becomes for you to channel your creativity into things that you are passionate about.

Creating a sense of self-awareness is critical in the exercise of your creative skills.

Living Outside of Your Bubble

"For me, insanity is super sanity. The normal is psychotic. Normal means lack of imagination, lack of creativity."

— Jean Dubuffet

If your goal is to foster creativity as a natural part of your life, it is necessary that you immerse yourself in an environment where such a goal can be met and realized. Creativity demands a dynamic environment where you are constantly engaged by the things that you see, hear, and feel. Without such dynamism, it would be very difficult, if not altogether impossible, to unleash your potential to be creative.

A good writer, for example, isn't content with just sitting behind a desk all day, typing away words as if devoid of context. It is often said that the best writers are those who try to experience things, those who are unafraid to get out of their comfort zones, all in the name of living life before eventually distilling it into words. All told, there is wisdom and greater depth in writing about things you have actually felt and experienced as opposed to things that you have merely conjured up in your head.

The same principle applies in other creative pursuits. If you want to have a wider perspective of things and gain a wealth of experience to draw inspiration from, it is necessary that you get yourself out there and take in as much insight as you can. How? Here are a number of ways to get you started with learning how to get out of your comfort zone:

Don't stop learning.

Read as many books as you can, watch as much stuff as you can, and listen to as much music as you can. Allot time to do any of these things to keep your mind from going stagnant. You want your imagination to work on overdrive, not remain static. The worst thing that can happen to you is when your head goes blank when asked to come up with something.

Many artists and intellectuals are consummate learners. These people are keenly aware of the fact that in order for them to be better at what they do, they need to keep themselves abreast of the news and trends both within and beyond their respective fields. This is precisely the reason why things such as continuing education and professional skills trainings are still offered. It is to ensure that you make improvements on, rather than completely unlearn, your skills.

Get on the road.

Exploring places and appreciating cultures different from yours constitutes an enriching way to learn and experience new things. Traveling is often said to be a self-rewarding exercise in that you pick up valuable lessons along the way. These lessons can either be realizations about yourself and the things you see around or the people you interact with.

When traveling, make it a point to be particularly observant. If possible, bring along a small notebook and a pen so that you can write down your thoughts while on the road. Be especially mindful of the scents you smell, the culinary fare you get to try out, the destinations you see, and the nuances of the culture you immerse yourself in. Try to make the whole thing a sensory experience. Inspiration will come sooner or later.

Meet new people.

While it is true that spending some alone time induces creativity, the same is true when you are in the company of other people. So instead of shying away from social situations, treat these as learning opportunities.

See, part of nurturing creativity is the ability to share knowledge and possibly collaborate with others. Learn from the people you interact with and impart insights to others, too. You will realize that fresh perspectives or ideas different from yours work wonders in defining your own perspective of things.

The fact is, the collaborative aspect of creativity is integral not only in the completion of big-scale projects, such as filming a full-length feature or designing a building, but is more particularly integral in the actual learning process. This is best exemplified by children working together on an arts and craft project, which teaches them the values of mutual respect and team work on top of the usual need to exercise creativity.

Creativity is fostered by engaging yourself in new insights and experiences beyond your comfort zone.

Understanding the Perils of Perfectionism

"Have no fear of perfection, you'll never reach it."

– Salvador Dali

Nothing is more attractive than the idea of perfection. It's certainly a beautiful thing to consider, especially when it comes to the fulfillment of your creative ideas. Of course, you want these ideas to turn out perfectly, so much so that achieving something short of perfect is not good enough.

Part of our fascination with perfection lies in its inherent impossibility. At the same time, it also has something to do with our own imperfect nature, where striving for perfection ultimately becomes a way of transcending our own imperfections.

However, is there such a thing as perfection? Conventional wisdom tells us there isn't, and the closest you could get to achieving it lies in giving your all in every pursuit you choose to undertake.

As such, the idea of perfection is a myth. The concept itself is not only unattainable; it is unsustainable, too. For instance, after having achieved perfection, what else would there be to strive for? Perfection signifies the zenith of success from which there is no other way to go but down. If you are striving to foster a culture of creativity in your life, you would want a constant state of growth and development, not to get stuck in a place where you are left to do nothing while basking in a delusional sense of triumph.

Given its unattainability, to subscribe to the notion of perfection, therefore, is to set yourself up for failure and disappointment. The more you strive for it, the more you realize how impossible it is to achieve it. The more disillusioned you are, the harder it becomes to motivate yourself to keep going and to keep your creative juice flowing.

Here are other reasons why perfectionism is not an ideal mindset to sport insofar as developing your creativity is concerned:

Perfectionism creates completely unnecessary tension and stress. When everything you or others do is not always up to your unreasonable standards, you are in effect raising the stress level not only for yourself but for others, too. When will these standards be met? Probably never, so there's that.

Perfectionism stifles your creative growth. You want nothing less than perfect, so obviously you leave little room for spontaneity, which is a key element of being creative. You tend to be overly cautious of everything you are doing, even to the point of micromanaging the most insignificant details. In this sense, cautiousness becomes your guiding principle—something that isn't really helpful at all in promoting greater creativity.

Aiming for perfection can be very self-limiting. When you refuse to entertain things that you think will not lead to perfection, you are essentially shutting off opportunities that may help you in the future.

Being a perfectionist takes away the fun in what you do and eventually breeds unhappiness. Being creative should be fun, engaging, and mentally stimulating, not scary and terrorizing. When the fear of failure and coming up short of your personal expectations becomes the rule in your life, dissatisfaction and guilt come about as the likely results. Where's the fun in that?

In sum, your sense of creativity should not be stifled by a misplaced sense of perfection. At the very least, your goals and expectations should be tempered by an ample dose of realism and reasonableness. There is nothing wrong in exacting high standards to yourself and your capabilities, unless these standards become the very same reason that brings you unhappiness, self-doubt, and the inability to grow.

Striving for perfection in your creative pursuits limits your growth and sets you up for disappointment. The best way to foster creativity is by allowing yourself to grow through your mistakes and by giving your best shot in everything you do.

Aiming for Sustainability

"You can't use up creativity. The more you use, the more you have."

– Maya Angelou

The thing about creativity is that it needs to be sustainable. This means that it should become an integral part of your life over the long term and not just over a brief period of time. The more deeply rooted creativity is in your life, the greater its impact becomes.

So how do you exactly make creativity an integral part of your day to day life? Here are a few important pointers to remember:

Embrace creativity as part of your life.

From the clothes you choose to wear to the way you design your apartment, almost all aspects of your life entails varying degrees of creativity. As such, there is actually very little excuse to not exercise your creative skills. But instead of treating these instances as chores you need to get done and over with, a better approach would be to take them as valuable learning opportunities.

Allot part of your schedule for some alone time.

Many experts argue that you are at your most creative when you are alone. When there are no other people around to disrupt your thoughts, you become in touch with your ideas and concepts. Make it a point to allocate time, even for only an hour, each day for you to be alone with yourself. This is a great way to foster discipline and to render a sense of regularity to your creativity sessions.

Learn the value of collaboration.

Even if you spend some time to be alone with your thoughts, do not completely disregard the value of collaboration. Being with other like-minded individuals is a great way to stimulate creativity and lend more fun to the actual activities. Remember that exercising creativity need not be very academic, and practicing it with other people guarantees that it will become a dynamic and an engaging experience.

Keep a journal.

If you want to keep track of your progress, keeping a journal is definitely the way to go. Writing down your thoughts, ideas, insights, and the actions you've taken to concretize your ideas allows you to assess how much you have learned and how much more effort you need to give to be better.

Indeed, creativity is something that you should learn to integrate in your day to day activities. It is only by doing so will it become deeply entrenched in your psyche.

Embracing creativity as part of your life is crucial in ensuring its sustainability.

Promoting a Healthy Body for a Healthy Mind

"There is no time for cut-and-dried monotony. There is time for work. And time for love. That leaves no other time."

– Coco Chanel

You have probably come across the idea of the starving artist—a broke, physically frail, and emotionally tortured soul yearning for nothing more than to create art that will encapsulate his or her inner struggles. Although largely bleak, this image romanticizes poverty and hunger as if these two concepts were requisites in inspiring creativity.

But now is as good a time as any to debunk this notion. For the fact is, fostering creativity does not only require a healthy sense of imagination. More importantly, it demands a sound physical state, which is essential if you want to optimize your potentials.

Consider this: how will it be possible to sustain your creativity if you are in a bad physical form? Even at schools, the emphasis on having healthy bodies through healthy lifestyle choices is underscored to all students. It should be no different for adults.

At the end of the day, you are able to think well and be on the top of your game if you are in great physical shape. You end up having more energy to do things, think clearly, and take concrete measures designed to bring your ideas into reality.

Kick starting a healthy lifestyle

Thankfully, there are a lot of things that you can do to kick start a healthy lifestyle, beginning of course with the quality of your dietary intake. The key lies in moderation. Avoid overeating, or conversely, eating too little. Watch out for the kind of food you consume. Make sure you don't end up eating food items that contain excessive amounts of cholesterol, sodium, MSG, and salt. Strive to achieve the required daily calorie intake for adults.

Closely related to having balanced meals is the need to do away with unhealthy habits, such as smoking and binge drinking. Smoking is a highly addictive activity that poses serious risks to your overall health condition. The same is true with drinking too much, which increases your chances of acquiring a number of gastro-intestinal disorders.

Complement your healthy dietary intake with a physically active lifestyle. The less sedentary you are, the better. As such, allot part of your schedule for regular workouts and adhere to it. Remember that you should be disciplined and committed enough to stick to your regular workouts.

You can work out either at the comfort of your own home or at a gym. At home, you get a greater sense of comfort and ease because you are already familiar with the environment. At the same time, you can multitask and do other tasks while working out. Just make sure to do proper research on the exercises you intend to carry out to make sure they match your immediate needs.

On the other hand, working out at the gym provides you access to pieces of equipment and tools to help you achieve your fitness goals. A certified fitness instructor is also on hand to assist you in coming up with a personalized workout routine designed to address your physical needs.

Confidence-booster

The importance of working out couldn't be emphasized enough. While having regular workouts boosts your stamina and improves your body's defenses against infections and diseases, its benefits are not merely limited to your overall physical condition. In fact, numerous studies point out that having a healthy body allows you to feel better about yourself, and is therefore instrumental in the development of self-confidence and a more solid sense of self-worth.

Aside from working out, do take time to engage in sports and outdoor recreational activities too. Taking part in sports not only enhances your physical form and sharpens your mental focus, it also fosters discipline and sportsmanship—valuable lessons that you can certainly apply in your quest to be more creative in your life.

Similarly, devoting part of your time for outdoor recreational activities can be a reinvigorating exercise. These activities provide for moments of introspection, which can be very useful in conjuring up ideas. Communing with nature is also a great way to draw much-needed inspiration.

Inspiring creativity requires not just a healthy mind, but also a healthy body.

Doing Away with the Fear of Failure

"Creativity is allowing yourself to make mistakes. Art is knowing which ones to keep."

— Scott Adams

Have you ever found yourself hesitating to embark on a project because you were afraid you would mess it up? Have you passed up on opportunities because you were convinced you weren't good enough for them? Have you given up on the notion that you are capable of great things?

If you answered in the affirmative to any of the questions above, then you may be harboring a debilitating fear of losing or failing.

In the course of inspiring greater creativity in your life, it is necessary, paramount even, to lose this sort of fear from your system. More than anything, this fear does nothing other than magnify the slim probability of failing, which should not really matter in the grand scheme of things. The more you entertain thoughts of failing, the tougher it gets for you to sport a positive outlook with regard to your capabilities.

Here are a few tricks to get over your fear of failing:

Don't pay too much attention to what others are saying or what you think they will say. Otherwise, you would be wasting your energy by dwelling on completely irrelevant things. Who cares what they think about you, right? Besides, these same folks are probably too busy with their own lives to bother themselves with your failures.

Improve your self-esteem. The fear of failure is often associated with an unhealthy sense of self. You probably think you are not skilled enough or that you are not smart enough to ever do anything significant. You're wrong. Practice positive reinforcement and believe that you have what it takes to succeed.

Sport a can-do attitude. If you think you can, then you can.

Stop looking at things around you as you would an exam. No one is out to castigate you in case you fail. Neither will there be anyone to call you out for missing the required mark. Loosen up and get rid of your inhibitions.

Start small and grow from there. Your fear of failure may be rooted in your unreasonable and unrealistic goals or expectations. If this is the case, learn to deal with small things first before branching out to bigger endeavors. If you have a hard time writing a novel, then maybe you can break it down to individual chapters first. This way you don't shock or scare yourself needlessly.

Learn to manage stress. When you are overpowered by stress, you lose the will to exercise creativity. Give yourself a break and take a breather if you must. Don't pressure yourself into doing something you have no way of completing. Gauge yourself and take action only once you feel you are ready.

Remember that your failures do not define you as a person. So learn to let go of your fear of failure in order to fully embrace a life of creativity.

The fear of failure can be very debilitating. In developing greater creativity, it is necessary to get rid of this fear.

Nurturing the Creative Spirit Over the Long Term

"Creativity is everything. It is the preview of life's coming attractions."

- Albert Einstein

As has been sufficiently underscored in the previous chapters, creativity is not a one-time exercise. To become deeply ingrained in your character, it has to be sustained over the long term. As such, it would do well for you to try to exercise your creative skills in everything you do.

Begin by dedicating a regular schedule for your creative pursuits. Doing so will help you get used to including creativity sessions in your daily itinerary. Regularity in exercising creativity is important because just as it is in any other field, such as sports, you need to put in time and effort to become better at what you are doing.

But regularity does not in any way imply predictability. Shake up your routine every now and then, particularly when you feel you are getting too comfortable with your routine. The key is to always find a reason to be excited.

Be in the company of creative people. Learn from them and be motivated with their work ethic, value to their skills, and capacity to exceed expectations. Take their experiences and successes as a springboard from which to launch your own creative pursuits.

Fun as motivation

Have fun, too. Being creative entails imagination and the ability to think outside of the box. Without the fun element, the entire process would seem bleak and too academic. Use fun as a motivation for you to keep going.

And finally, reward yourself. Although creativity by itself should serve as its own reward, it doesn't hurt to reinforce your commitment to be more creative by incentivizing your hard work and valuable time spent. In addition, this should not in any way be misconstrued as an act of vanity because it isn't. What this does is merely to motivate you to work harder and give your best shot every time.

So after finishing, say, an arts and craft project, treat yourself with life's little pleasures, such as a warm bath or a cup of cocoa. You can also allow yourself to take a break in order to relax and get yourself excited as you plan out your next project.

In sum, fostering greater creativity in your life is possible, particularly when you are disciplined and driven enough to succeed. When sustained over the long term, creativity can be very useful in defining your character and in turning your great ideas into reality.

So get yourself ready on this exciting journey to unleash your fullest potential. Now is as good a time as any to get started.

Boosting your creativity is not a one-time exercise. You should take measures to ensure your sense of creativity is nurtured over the long term.

How to Apply Key Ideas for the Best Results?

Although creativity is a skill that you can learn over time, know that it needs to be sustained and integrated into your day to day affairs so that it can really take root and become part of your life. Treat your failures as opportunities to learn and be better. Do not be afraid of them. At the same time, look at your successes as an affirmation of your discipline and commitment to your craft. Most importantly, treat creativity as a self-rewarding exercise. The more creative you become, the greater happiness you derive and the more meaningful your life becomes.

www.ingramcontent.com/pod-product-compliance
Lightning Source LLC
Chambersburg PA
CBHW070427190526
45169CB00003B/1446